Message to Parents

Congratulations on your child's participation in American Red Cross Lear an important part of your child's swimming experience. We encourage you a booklet together during this session. It includes:

- A story line that supports and reinforces what your child is learning.
- Progress reports that indicate your child's progress toward passing the Red Cross Learn-to-Swim Level 3—Stroke Development and Learn-to-Swim Level 4—Stroke Improvement. Your child's instructor will complete the progress reports at the end of the session.
- Activities to help you practice with your child.
- Tips for safe diving to help keep you and your family safe from injuries to the head, neck or back.
- Certificates of achievement that celebrate your child's success in Red Cross Learn-to-Swim. Cut the certificates out and hang them in a visible place in your home for all to see!
- A chart that provides an overview of Red Cross Learn-to-Swim.

You can play a role in helping your child learn to swim! You can help by:

- Providing for your child's safety around water at all times
- Maintaining enthusiasm and a positive attitude about learning to swim
- Ensuring that your child attends each swimming lesson
- Discussing and applying the water safety rules
- Practicing the fundamental skills your child is learning in class

Page 14 suggests activities to do with your child that reinforce what he or she is learning. At these levels, your child has basic aquatic skills, but there must always be adult supervision whenever your child is in the water.

A way to encourage practice is to simply ask your child to show you the skills he or she is learning in class. Your interest and enthusiasm for the progress your child is achieving is a great motivator! You can use the progress reports in this booklet as a prompt to remind your child and describe the skills if he or she has difficulty remembering. Also, talk with your child's instructor. The instructor can explain specific activities or drills that can help with any problem areas.

It is important to know that your child is learning head-first entries now. Your child must know rules of safe diving and where it is safe to dive.

It cannot be overemphasized that participation in any swimming lesson program will not "drownproof" your child. It is only the first step in developing your child's water safety and swimming skills. Year-round practice, regular exposure to water and positive encouragement are the tools needed for developing your child's comfort level in water and improving his or her swimming skills.

The Red Cross strongly recommends that a swimmer engage in water activities only where there is adult supervision. We also urge that your child's swimming and water safety education be continued by participating in all of the levels in Red Cross Learn-to-Swim.

Contact your local American Red Cross chapter for further information.

Waddles In The Deep

American Red Cross Learn-to-Swim Levels 3 and 4

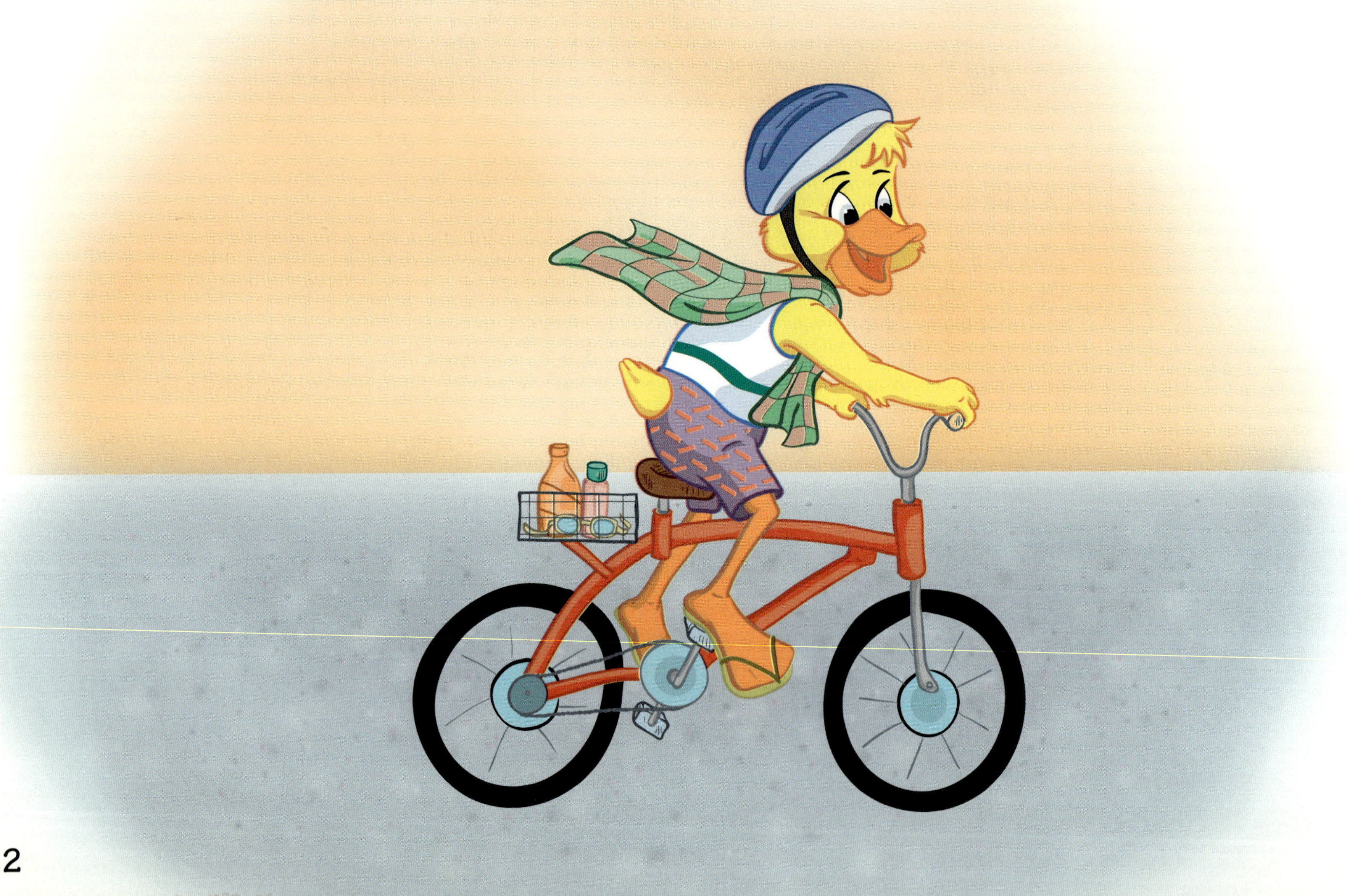

"Are you ready for swim lessons, Waddles?" asked Sophie Dog excitedly.

"I sure am!" answered Waddles. "I can't wait to learn to jump into deep water and do the butterfly! I'll see you there!" Waddles hung up the phone, grabbed his swim gear, jumped on his bike and headed for the pool.

Waddles met up with Sophie and the rest of the class at the pool. Mr. Casey Condor, the American Red Cross instructor, greeted the kids and introduced himself.

"My name is Mr. Casey Condor and you can call me Mr. Casey. Many of you have completed Levels 1 and 2 with Miss LaPink. Let's talk about some of the things you will be learning in Levels 3 and 4. You will learn how to jump and dive into the pool. You will also start to learn about all the strokes: the front crawl, the back crawl, butterfly, breaststroke, elementary backstroke and even the sidestroke."

Everyone's eyes got big as Mr. Casey talked.

"Oooh," and "Ahh," they said.

"Let's review some of the water safety rules we have already learned," said Mr. Casey. "Who can remember a rule?" Mr. Casey asked the class.

Waddles raised his hand and said, "Swim with a Buddy in a Supervised Area."

"That's right!" said Mr. Casey. "What's another rule?"

"Be Cool, Follow the Rules!" said Hatch Alligator proudly.

"Absolutely!" said Mr. Casey. "Let's keep talking about more rules for water safety. Another rule is: Think So You Don't Sink. How many of you have seen someone get in trouble in the water?"

Eddie Elephant raised his hand and said, "My cousin once got a cramp in her leg when swimming."

"That's a good example of getting into trouble," said Mr. Casey. "An important thing to remember when you get into trouble in the water is to stay calm. For example, when Eddie's cousin got a leg cramp, she should have relaxed and rubbed her cramped muscle."

"Mr. Casey, what should I do if I see someone in trouble in the water?" asked Waddles.

"If you see someone having trouble in the water, remember another rule: Reach or Throw, Don't Go! To be safe, either reach out from the side of the pool or throw him a rope, plastic bottle, a ball, a large branch or anything that floats. Then get help. Remember, do not try to get in the water and rescue someone by yourself!" said Mr. Casey.

"Let's practice."

"Great job everyone!" said Mr. Casey. "Now let's all get in the water and start swimming! We're going to keep working on strokes that you swim on your front. Does anyone know what the front crawl looks like?" he said.

"I do! I do!" shouted Waddles excitedly.

"Great! Everyone gets to practice," said Mr. Casey to the class.

As each student practiced, Mr. Casey helped them get better. They moved on to other strokes, including strokes on their backs! All of the students were getting better and better as they practiced more and more. Only from time to time did Sophie have some problems making her legs cooperate.

"Now let's get into the deep end of the pool by jumping from the side," said Mr. Casey.

Waddles was a bit nervous. He had only been in the deep end of the pool a few times and had never jumped in. He watched his other classmates jump right in with a splash and swim right back to the side of the pool. "On the count of three," he thought to himself, "I'll do it."

"One...two...three..." Waddles jumped into the pool and made even a bigger splash than Eddie Elephant.

He came out of the water with a huge smile! "I did it!" Waddles exclaimed.

"You can enter deep water in another way—starting with your fingertips, followed by your head and the rest of your body. Would anyone like to see how that looks?" asked Mr. Casey.

"Oh yes," the children replied in awe.

Mr. Casey extended his arms over his head, squeezing his ears tightly, and entered the water beautifully with very little splash. He came right back up to the surface of the water to hear all the children cheering.

"I want to try! I want to try!" was the chant of most of the students. But Mr. Casey noticed that Waddles was not chanting along with his class.

“Before anyone tries, let’s go over some rules for entering the water this way,” Mr. Casey told the class. “First, learn how to dive properly from a qualified instructor—that’s me. Obey all posted rules and ‘No Diving’ signs. Never, ever enter headfirst into shallow water or in above-ground pools,” he said.

“Okay, now it’s your turn!” said Mr. Casey. “We’re going to start off by sitting on the side. Everybody show me how to position your arms.”

All the kids lined up in a row at the edge of the pool with their arms extended, pointed toward the water.

“Everyone looks great! Now each one of you will take your first plunge!” exclaimed Mr. Casey. One by one, Waddles’ classmates entered the water, came up to the surface and swam back to the side.

Now it was Waddles turn. He was a bit nervous, but Mr. Casey moved so that he was right beside Waddles.

Mr. Casey said to Waddles, "Touch your fingers against my hands and follow my hands into the water."

This made Waddles feel very safe. So, he pushed off and entered the water, squeezing his ears as hard as he could. It was beautiful!

This gave him all the confidence he needed to keep practicing and become very good at entering deep water from all sorts of positions, including starting from his knees and even from standing on two feet.

On the last day of lessons with Mr. Casey, Waddles and Sophie and their classmates were very excited. On this day, they were going to show their parents how much they had learned.

Throughout the lesson, the students proudly demonstrated the many different things they could do in the water. The parents cheered wildly.

After the class was over, Waddles and his mother were leaving the pool. With a happy and proud look, Waddles asked his mother, "When do my next lessons start?"

Stroke Development

LEVEL 3

- ☐ Jump into deep water from the side
- ☐ Head-first entry from the side in a sitting or kneeling position

- ☐ Submerge and retrieve an object, 3 seconds
- ☐ Perform bobs with the head fully submerged, 5 times
- ☐ Perform rotary breathing with the body in a horizontal position, 5 times

- ☐ Front glide—kick one, 2 body lengths
- ☐ Front glide—kick two, 2 body lengths
- ☐ Survival float, 30 seconds
- ☐ Back glide—kick one, 2 body lengths
- ☐ Back glide—kick two, 2 body lengths
- ☐ Back float, 30 seconds

- ☐ Change from vertical to horizontal position on front, in deep water
- ☐ Change from vertical to horizontal position on back, in deep water
- ☐ Tread water, 30 seconds, in deep water

- ☐ Front crawl, 15 yards
- ☐ Butterfly—kick and body motion, 15 feet

- ☐ Back crawl, 15 yards

- ☐ General water safety rules
- ☐ Wearing a life jacket, enter the water using ladder, steps or side
- ☐ HELP position, 1 minute
- ☐ Huddle position, 1 minute
- ☐ Perform reaching assist
- ☐ Check-Call-Care

My Name: ______________________________

My Instructor: ___________________________

Date: ________________________________

Location: ______________________________

Exit Skills Assessment

☐ 1. Jump into chest-deep water from the side, swim front crawl for 15 yards with face in the water and rhythmic breathing pattern (to front or side), maintain position by treading or floating for 30 seconds and swim back crawl for 15 yards.

Stroke Improvement

LEVEL 4

- ☐ Dive from side in a compact or stride position

- ☐ Swim underwater, 3 body lengths
- ☐ Perform a feet-first surface dive and submerge completely

- ☐ Survival float, 1 minute, in deep water
- ☐ Back float, 1 minute, in deep water

- ☐ Open turn on front and push off in streamlined position
- ☐ Open turn on back and push off in streamlined position
- ☐ Tread water using modified scissors, breaststroke or rotary kick and sculling arm motions, 1 minute

- ☐ Front crawl, 25 yards
- ☐ Breaststroke, 15 yards
- ☐ Butterfly, 15 yards

- ☐ Back crawl, 25 yards
- ☐ Elementary backstroke, 15 yards
- ☐ Swim on side with scissors kick, 15 yards

- ☐ Additional rules for safe diving
- ☐ Compact jump into the water from a height while wearing a life jacket
- ☐ Throwing assist
- ☐ Care for conscious choking victim

My Name: ____________________

My Instructor: ____________________

Date: ____________________

Location: ____________________

Exit Skills Assessment

- ☐ 1. Perform a feet-first entry into chest-deep water, swim front crawl for 25 yards, maintain position on back for 1 minute in deep water (float or sculling) and swim elementary backstroke for 15 yards.
- ☐ 2. Swim breaststroke for 15 yards, tread water for 1 minute and swim back crawl for 25 yards.

Helping Your Child Progress

Safety Tour

Take your child on a guided tour of the swimming area. Explain the rules of the swimming area. Be sure your child knows that the swimming area is off limits unless an adult is present to supervise. Also, be sure to review the diving safety rules that are included in this booklet. Stress to your child where it is safe to dive and be clear about where diving is prohibited.

Entering the Water

Hands Down, Hands Out, Hands Up—Have your child jump from the edge of the pool into deep water. As your child begins to jump, shout out one of the following phrases:

- Hands down: Child enters the water with his or her hands below the hips
- Hands out: Child enters the water with his or her hands at shoulder level
- Hands up: Child enters the water with his or her hands above the head

Submersion and Underwater Exploration

Egg Hunt—Fill different colored plastic eggs with about 10 pennies. It may be necessary to tape the seams. Drop the eggs into different depths of water, depending on your child's ability. Begin in shallow water. As your child gains confidence and skill, drop the eggs into deeper depths. Tell your child that on your command, he or she is to submerge and gather as many eggs as possible in the color that you call out. Repeat until all the eggs have been gathered.

Underwater Swimming

Underwater Obstacle Course—Have your child swim through a series of hoops that are placed underwater. As your child improves, increase the distance between the hoops. For safety, make sure that the hoops are placed away from the wall so that your child does not strike the wall while swimming, and do not let your child hyperventilate.

Streamline off the Wall—Place a large hula-hoop 2 to 3 body lengths away from the wall. Have your child push off the wall and swim through the hoop while maintaining a streamlined position. Repeat using a hula-hoop of smaller diameter. Repeat the activity, each time using a hoop of smaller diameter, to see how small of a hoop your child can go through without touching the sides.

Gliding

Blasting Off—Have your child pretend to be a rocket ship. Have him or her extend the hands over the head and place a foot on the side of pool. Begin a countdown and on your cue, have your child blast off. To blast off, your child puts the face and arms in the water, the other foot on the side and pushes off. Vary the activity by having your child swim on the front and back and add kicks for the "engine booster."

Kicking

Soft Kick, Hard Kick—Have your child bracket on the wall on the front with the legs extended. When you say "Soft Kick," have your child flutter kick as slow and with as small of a kick as possible. When you say "Hard Kick," have your child flutter kick as hard as possible. Repeat 2 or 3 times. Have your child rotate so he or she is bracketed on one side with the legs extended. Repeat the cycle until your child rotates to the back, the other side and then back to the front. As your child's confidence and ability improve, he or she can use a kickboard with this drill.

Combined Skills

Talking to the Fish—Using a kickboard, have your child put his or her face in the water and use any kick. With the face in the water, have your child pretend to be talking to the fish. The child talks to the fish by exhaling and blowing bubbles. The child listens to the fish by turning the face to the side so that the ear is in the water.

Simon Says—Tell your child that you are going to call out skills, such as treading water or front crawl. Explain that if you say the words, Simon Says, he or she should do the skills that you say. Explain that if you do not say the words, Simon Says, he or she should not move. Consult the progress log for skills.

Learn-to-Swim

Stroke Improvement

Name ______________________________

Facility Name ______________________

Date ______________________________

____

Instructor Signature

LEVEL 4

Learn-to-Swim

Stroke Development

Name ______________________________

Facility Name ______________________

Date ______________________________

____

Instructor Signature

LEVEL 3

Diving Safety

A head-first entry into shallow water is the leading cause of head, neck or back injuries in the water. The following guidelines are recommended for safe diving:

- Learn how to dive safely from a qualified instructor.
- In a head-first dive, extend the arms with your elbows locked alongside the head. Keep your hands together with thumbs touching (or interlocked) and palms facing toward the water. Keeping the arms, wrists and fingers in line with the head helps control the angle of entry. This reduces the impact of the water on the top of the head and helps protect from injury. A diver's body should be tensed and straight from the hands to the pointed toes.
- Follow safety rules at all times—never make exceptions.
- Do not wear earplugs; pressure changes make them dangerous.
- Obey "No Diving" signs. They are there for safety.
- Be sure of water depth and ensure that the water is free from obstructions. The first time in the water, ease in or walk in; do not jump or dive.
- Never dive into an above-ground pool, the shallow end of any in-ground pool or at a beach.
- Never dive into cloudy or murky water.
- In open water, always check first for objects under the surface, such as logs, stumps, boulders and pilings.
- Check the shape of the pool bottom to be sure the diving area is large enough and deep enough for the intended dive.
- The presence of a diving board does not necessarily mean it is safe to dive. Pools at homes, motels and hotels might not have a safe diving envelope.
- When diving from a deck, the area of entry should be free of obstructions (such as lane lines and kickboards) for at least 4 feet on both sides. For dives from a 1-meter diving board, you need 10 feet of clearance on both sides.
- Dive only off the end of a diving board. Diving off the side of a diving board might result in striking the side of the pool or entering water that is not deep enough.
- Do not bounce more than once on the end of a diving board to avoid missing the edge or slipping off the diving board.
- Do not run on a diving board or attempt to dive a long way through the air. The water might not be deep enough at the point of entry.
- For springboard diving, use equipment that meets the standards set for competition.
- Do not dive from a height greater than 1 meter unless trained in elevated entry.
- Swim away from the diving board after entering the water. Do not be a hazard for the next diver.
- Never use drugs or alcohol when diving.

Life Jackets

- Anyone who cannot swim well should wear or have a life jacket if they are going to be in, on or around the water.
- Even good swimmers should wear a life jacket when boating or water skiing or if there is any chance of falling or being thrown into the water.
- Although you should always wear your life jacket, it is even more important when the water temperature is cold.
- The U.S. Coast Guard has arranged personal flotation devices into five types. The four wearable types may have permanent flotation or may be inflatable.
  - Type I (offshore life jackets): They turn most unconscious wearers in the water from a face-down position to a vertical or slightly tipped-back position.
  - Type II (near shore): They may help turn an unconscious person in the water from a face-down position to a vertical or slightly tipped-back position. Type II life jackets have less buoyancy than type I life jackets but are more comfortable to wear.
  - Type III (flotation aids): These "float coats" or vests may keep a conscious person in a vertical or slightly tipped-back position. Type III is more comfortable for active water sports than types I and II.
  - Type IV (throwable devices): Flotation devices, such as a buoyant cushion or the ring buoy, are not worn but can be thrown to a victim in an emergency. A buoyant cushion may be used as a seat cushion. These devices do not take the place of wearing a life jacket.
  - Type V (restricted-use life jacket): These special purpose devices are approved for specific activities, such as commercial whitewater rafting and riding personal watercraft, where other types of life preserver devices would be too constrictive or when more protection is needed.

When choosing a life jacket:

- Make sure it is the right type for the right activity.
- Make sure it is approved by the U.S. Coast Guard.
- Make sure it fits the intended user. Check the stamp on the life jacket for weight limits.
- Make sure it is in good condition. Check buckles and straps for proper function. Discard any life jacket with torn fabric or loose straps.
- Practice putting it on in water and swimming with it on. When you practice, have a companion with you who can help you if you have difficulty.

What Not to Use

Inflatables, such as water wings, swim rings and other flotation devices, are not designed to be used as substitutes for U.S. Coast Guard–approved life jackets or life vests or adult supervision. Swimmers may go beyond their ability and fall off the inflatable, which may lead to a drowning situation. Inflatable materials deteriorate in sun and rough pool surfaces leading to deflation and leaks.